The City as Modern Mausoleum

poems by

Peter Faziani

Finishing Line Press
Georgetown, Kentucky

The City as Modern Mausoleum

Copyright © 2019 by Peter Faziani
ISBN 978-1-64662-082-1 First Edition
All rights reserved under International and Pan-American Copyright Conventions. No part of this book may be reproduced in any manner whatsoever without written permission from the publisher, except in the case of brief quotations embodied in critical articles and reviews.

ACKNOWLEDGMENTS

The City as Indentured Teeth first published in *The Qua*

Publisher: Leah Maines
Editor: Christen Kincaid
Cover Art and Design: Sarah Everett
Author Photo: Ellyn Faziani

Printed in the USA on acid-free paper.
Order online: www.finishinglinepress.com
                also available on amazon.com

                        Author inquiries and mail orders:
                              Finishing Line Press
                                P. O. Box 1626
                          Georgetown, Kentucky 40324
                                    U. S. A.

Table of Contents

The City as Cemetery Plots 1

The City Skyline as Indentured Teeth 2

The City as Modern 3

Bones Buried on Bones 4

The Night Life between Bricks 5

Tired Metaphors Best Describe the City 6

A Little Boozie and One More Drink to Go 7

Chance, Lore, and Feigning a Middle-Class Salary 8

The City from Above 9

Sky Scraper Tongue Brush 10

A Mythical Constant Deep Between the Brick and Mortar 11

The City's VMA Speech 12

Castrating the Past 13

The Family Secret 14

Going and Going 15

Upon Listening to Minus the Bear's "What About the Boat"? 16

Secret Living Reveals Real Truth 17

Cash Burns Pockets 18

Time Served 19

When the City Meets a Doppelgänger, or, Needling the City 20

The Signs of the Times are Blank and Blaming 21

The City is a Bar Post 2004 22

Burning the Back Catalog 23

These Birds Don't have Wings 24

The City Doesn't Trust My Ever-Thin Pocket Book 25

Like Everything Else, this is for E.

"The mind balks and the mind breaks"

—Andrew Field, "The Relationship Between Nouns and Verbs," *All I Want*

The City as Cemetery Plots

there's corpse in 17b
a wife and mother reduced to
memories reduced to carbon
a copse of trees shade her from
the Big S son
in memoriam the son says
her city life was dictated in distance
coordinates plotable in minutes
her walk to work
a bicycle ride to the local grocer
        a middle-class haven with shelves stocked
        and expiration dates clearly marked
trips to the park
        the one with his favorite red slide
        or the swings that hadn't been broken
        yet
the full-time position that she fought
        tooth and nail sans
        college degree to get

The City Skyline as Indentured Teeth

rows of uneven brick
on and on forever
unending inhabitants
the bones of the mouth of the world
cavernous and carnivorous
chew and swallow and dreams
forsaken to pay constant upkeep
rebuilding and renewing because
gentrification is a mouthful when you're
suckling on a white collar

The City as Modern

a building
        any building
maybe the one you see in
syndicated episodes of Friends
or Seinfeld or the Jeffersons
not the Jetsons
        never the Jetsons
                those boujie bastards

bodies rest
because on earth there's a law
one I never agreed to—but it says that
bodies in motion tend to stay in motion
until they're not
and in these buildings
they're not

Doritos bags and cheese dust
layer the coffee table
rabbit ears wearing McDonald's
cups stacked and sticky with
sugary residue—an American ideal

the television airs episodes
all hours of the day
Sandford and Lamont
a childhood without cable but we had a
nice view
of the graffiti on an adjacent building

Bones Buried on Bones

there's a city beneath the city
artifice history buried
an attempt to forget
the bones
the artifacts
the million-year memory
man digs deeper to build up
new crypts in the latest fad
glamorizing the way we forget
femurs
        bricks
                pottery
storied murderers suspected
the city beneath the city
houses the dead as if dead never existed

The Night Life Between Bricks

stray cats stay husbands
and the alley shadows are
always a few inches too short
to disguise genuine dissatisfaction

the city hides the skeletons
under the bridges
in the ashes of the burns
in the bodies of the bums

the city at night echoes
broken careers and bandit spouses

Tired Metaphors Best Describe the City

rats
maze
holy like swiss
but there's a truth
a test subject
subhuman today
tomorrow's cancer
cutting out the violence
in the body the city's teeth draws blood
a needle in prime time
privately placed

A Little Boozie and One More Drink to Go

the city smells wounded and offended
a bird with a broken wing in the rain
left the nest unprepared and
against parental advice because
nonorganic twice chewed worms were wrong
in the city ever innocent birds squawk
from the highest soapbox their underpaid salary can buy
a solidarity in squalor
reeking of a little mildew and
a little wild
a little boozie of their
faux boujie lifestyle
slumming between months
of unpaid rent
capitalizing on their stock by sharing
cheap cans of PBR

Chance, Lore, and Feigning a Middle-Class Salary

penthouse occupants
with guttered mindsets and
seven figures view
from upon high
that way the peons look
like ants as
the city slinks

middle-class lies sewn into
a wearing suit but it's the monogrammed cuffs
that give you up

the air is thinning and
the view is cathartic in
forgetting the bodies
buried to get here

The City from Above

the second hour
after getting high
distinctly familiar but distant
broken
much like a father-son relationship
that might've existed between Icarus and Daedalus
today
on the ground he looks up into the tunnel vision
the cement paradise barricaded by the steel
glass
ghosts
where does the penny go when thrown from the top?
Icarus knows all too well and Daedalus isn't ready to talk about it

Sky Scraper Tongue Brush

the city sours my mouth
a chemical reaction
mechanical halitosis
consequence of the stainless
the glass
decades of CFC's from
rooftop units cooling penthouse oxygen
in late January blizzards
manufacturers of fresh air warn
to avoid direct contact with skin
as if the city offered a place to escape
a place to hide

A Mythical Constant Deep Between the Brick and Mortar

the city is a fire breather
hot breath down the base
of my neck
the city makes me
sweat long to be clean
long for Christ in this
false Galilee
skeletal secrets
manifest by the million
the believers just as much as
those that don't
where a femur becomes a
bludgeon
a glutton your neighbor

The City's VMA Speech

the city soundtrack
a raucous collection of
horn muzak keeping time
to the rumble of
tire rubber melting into
layered asphalt
the bodies drown it out
the background noise
the screeches the squawks
the indiscernible lack of birds
and the bloody pleas for help
the city can't help
what it refuses to hear

the city heard the miracle of
portable music and never went back

Castrating the Past

the city echoes with anonymity
a cacophonal bellow reverberating
between channels
and charnels
tear through as the wind does
to the leaves on what few leaves
those city trees have left
but still I will scream
until I'm drowning in echoes
of the city's other versions of me

The Family Secret

the city has secret
teeth hidden beneath
the gum line in old
crumbling sites of wisdom
a history forsaken and torn out
in the name of upward mobility
so make more space

the city has secret
sharp edged weapons targeting
the rural targeting the
suburban tearing the
flesh from the bone from
the muscle from the memory of
the mouth freed
from the city

Going and Going

the city sleepwalks
a marathon outside time
the bodily populous moving
veins and streets intermingle
blood tinged c02
no winners without scars
mid shin roughly
a bumpers height
the movement is a race
to beat the grand
father that died before you
turned three
a race to do better than
his father before him
back when the city
wasn't a race but a mosey

Upon Listening to Minus the Bear's "What About the Boat"?

the city is collision in perpetuity
heads out hands first
chin up the paralysis is permanent
hands grasping for hope
useless
unless someone is sacrificed
the guillotine has a price
profit in place of bound necks
bound hands
perfunctory stampedes
look down upon your dead
meet eyes withholding hands
look down at your dying
wavering thoughts and stray eyes
lift your corpses
in the name of everything wrong
with anyone else
ringed fingers wag accusingly
ignorant to the blood they used to polish
expensive shoe leathers
pretending complacency is unintentional

Secret Living Reveals Real Truth

the city is habitual
motion sans meaning
people 86'd a purpose
soulless bodies that wanted
to be actors
        executives
                etcetera because the broken dreams
number too many
to remember but please
the city wants to forget
a memory etched in acids
bile and vomit
prisoners on the lamb
from the chain
train
but untrained
because no one comes to the city
to be a barista

Cash Burns Pockets

the city is more than a place
a mentality succumbing to illness
justified serialist
a thirst for succession
if not here then soon
an ideology of times to come
cash paper lining cuffs
and pant suits because
misogyny runs rampant
an unframed reference
offers easy inference
that city sex sells
to the people outside
the city limits

Time Served

the city has been stripped naked and forced
to forgo dreams of ability and
achievement that Truslow Adams
once called for
caged in by
nepotistic values
all in the family
the family is all in
buyers and sellers share a wealth
where workers bid for time away from forgotten cellars

When the City Meets a Doppelgänger, or, Needling the City

people in the city walking the same streets
come face to face with culture
face to face with swine
a mouthful of vile
a two-star hotel
dens of vice because
the culture isn't welcome uptown
and the creators have to eat and drink
somewhere so the city serves
reds
    cabs
        and absinthe with steel reserve
chasers
chasing the wealth into the drains
the city corrals residents to prevent
mingling up
but with the right money you can sink
into the cultured slums

The Signs of the Times are Blank and Blaming

the city is wound around
a wound of mazes
one for each activist
a trap to give you meaning
as if the cheese on the other end
actually gave a damn
signs on signs on signs
unsigned a paper cut of resistance
claiming political normalcy
amazed maze a view from above
what's your cause got to do with this
city the tour bus calls to the thousand people
with the might of mice

The City is a Bar Post 2004

where cigarettes are banned and
vaping isn't a thing
yet
still unknown
yet to be outlawed

the stale smoke on my jacket
makes it vintage
something my dad might have worn in the 70s
after Vietnam and shooting up
before finding peace in a 30 pack

hiding its memory in my pocket
a wrinkled phone number on an old photograph
 washed and washed and washed
but still able to be read because
mother taught me never to dry jean
and the dryers cost too much

I like my jackets like I like my friends
stiff

a night out drinking well and domestic
the special ends at 11 and its 11:01
What happened to the Millennial Last Call?

Burning the Back Catalog

all those songs you wish
your favorite band never released
echo from downed sedan windows
but when you listen to the back catalog any
song will do
the tonal appropriations of strings on
pick-ups and effects ring true
a cd with poor reviews
it's dusk and summer all year
the city can't wait for the follow up
a return to true
but the rhythm is a constant
that's ever changing in favor of profit

These Birds Don't have Wings

secrets hidden in plain sight
the monuments and memories
erected in the name of a t-rex in a cardigan
with an arm up Friday

bricked sidewalks uneven
the red clay
cantankerously shouting
as hipsters in trendy fashions
shirt dresses in winter
the snow upskirt
chapped skin

the signatures of the architects
hide in cornerstones
to be forgotten as twenty-somethings
emojize their feelings for the present
whilst neon bulbs historicize the realities
showing an ignorance to the truth

Peter Faziani is the founding editor of *Red Flag Poetry*, a journal sponsored by Indiana University of Pennsylvania that publishes poetry postcards. His poetry has been published by *Rising Phoenix Review, Silver Birch Press, Sandy River Review, The Tau, Ocean State Review, The Qua, Garfield Lake Review*, and others. His first book of poetry, *Warning Shots*, was published by Words Dance Publishing in 2017. He is currently teaching at Central Michigan University.

www.ingramcontent.com/pod-product-compliance
Lightning Source LLC
LaVergne TN
LVHW041520070426
835507LV00012B/1707